DON'T BE A
nordic

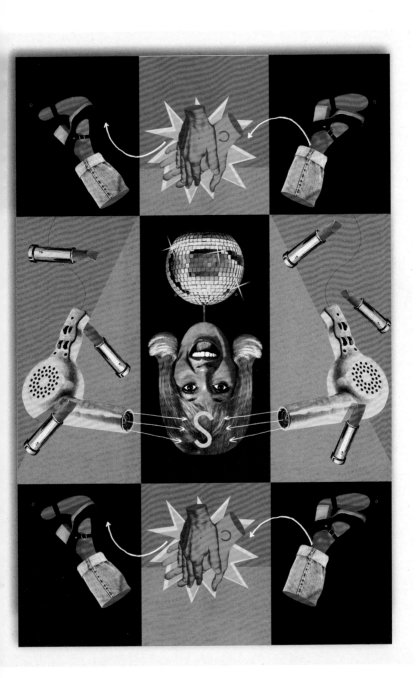

DON'T BE A
nordic

WHY EMBRACING THE SCANDI LIFESTYLE
WON'T CHANGE YOUR LIFE

JO HOARE

DOG 'n' BONE

Published in 2017 by Dog 'n' Bone Books
An imprint of Ryland Peters & Small Ltd
20–21 Jockey's Fields   341 E 116th St
London WC1R 4BW   New York, NY 10029

www.rylandpeters.com

10 9 8 7 6 5 4 3 2 1

Text © Jo Hoare 2017
Design and illustration © Dog 'n' Bone Books 2017

A CIP catalog record for this book is available from the
Library of Congress and the British Library.

ISBN: 978 1 911026 29 7

Printed in China

Designer: Emily Breen
Illustrator: Blair Frame

CONTENTS

6   Introduction

A LOOK AT ALL THINGS NORDIC

10   How Nordic are You?

12   Is H & M Trying to Take Over the World?

14   Canvas Backpacks

16   Men's Turtlenecks and Snoods

18   Scandinavian Music

22   Ice-white Hair

24   Nordic Icons

30   Yes or No-rdic?

32   The 10 Worst Things About Being a Nordic

36   Weird Nordic Hobbies

38   Scandi-phile Checklist: the Five Products Only the Dedicated Will Own

40   Calling BS on Hygge

43   Nordic Food: Some Questions

46   The Case Against Lagom

48   Seven Scandi-inspired Interior Decisions You've Probably Made and Why They Were a Mistake

52   Sex: What's the Deal?

54   The Downside of Nordic Noir TV

56   Scandi Things There's No Point In Trying To Get Away With IRL

60   What's Next for Nordic Fans?

64   Index

INTRODUCTION

Remember when you didn't even know what Nordic really meant, when it was just a word you associated with Vikings and maybe a god or two that you learnt about at school? (FYI, it's perfectly acceptable to admit you still don't know what Nordic means, because the Nordic-ization of culture has got us all mixed up. Who knew that, politically, Iceland and Finland aren't part of Scandinavia, but for the purpose of selling you a bed/burger/ lifestyle they definitely are Scandinavian? Anyway, we digress.) PNP (pre-Nordic proliferation), trips to Copenhagen, Oslo, and Stockholm were strictly the preserve of those annoying people you met at university who had been Interrailing around Europe and had a different photo album for each city, with a special compartment to display used train tickets.

Fast forward a decade and if we're not all jetting off there for a *Midsomer* crayfish party or a hike around the fjords, then we're creating our own little Nordic fiefdom at home, building a fortress out of sheepskin rugs, fake fur throws, IKEA sofas, and Scandi-Noir box sets. But WHY? With self-acknowledged reputations for being boring, and having high suicide and depression rates, serious alcohol problems, and about five minutes daylight a year, at first glance the Scandi countries don't appear to be the most aspirational. Is it really all down to our obsession with their TV shows about complicated police officers on a journey of their own in a nice jumper/parka/suit? Is it IKEA's fault, or can we lay blame at the door of New Nordic Cuisine? TBH, it's probably

Instagram's fault. Sure, beach shots are cool and changing-room selfies are sadly probably always going to be a thing, but for real look-at-me social-media impact, a Northern Light here, a picturesque mountain hike or waist-deep snow there is always going to get a pause and, fingers crossed guys, a like!

Worried you're not quite *au fait* (apologies for the French word—we tried for a Scandi alternative, really we did) with the whole Nordic world? Well, you've come to the right place... From the icons you need to know about and the food you really wish you didn't know about, to how to wear your snood and what Scandi sex is really like (the two may be related), this book covers it all. *Varsågod.*

A LOOK AT ALL THINGS NORDIC

HOW NORDIC ARE YOU?

A Scandinavian obsession can be a dangerous thing (a bit like a trip to IKEA during sales season—the opening of a London store resulted in a stampede for bargain Billy bookcases that saw six flat-pack lovers hospitalized). It starts innocently enough—the purchase of a Fair Isle sweater here, a trip to see an exhibition on Scandinavian design there—but soon you've filled your home with countless folk-art trinkets, enough cozy pillows, throws, and blankets to ensure that even the Princess and the Pea could get a good night's sleep, and you've just had the planning permission accepted for your own wind turbine in the backyard. So just how deep is your love of all things Nordic? Take this quiz and find out.

Are you actually from Sweden, Denmark, Norway, Iceland, or Finland?
A) Yes.
B) No, but I've been on two weekend breaks to Copenhagen and I've just used my Avios points for a flight to Gothenberg next month.
C) No, but I think my shower curtain is from IKEA.

We say ABBA, you say...
A) You mean Auntie Agnetha?
B) I once broke my ankle dancing to Waterloo at a wedding.
C) An example of a palindrome?

Do you suffer from SAD?
A) No way! Candlelight is much more of a mood-lifting illuminator than the overrated sunshine.
B) I definitely need a week or two on a beach occasionally.

C) Terribly, I have three light-therapy lamps next to my bed. In high summer.

How do you feel about taxes?
A) High taxes are essential for a happy country.
B) Well, I might have put the odd dodgy taxi receipt in my tax return once or twice in the past.
C) That PO box in the Cayman Islands is my best friend.

Do you own a cheese slicer?
A) Do you mean an *osthyvel*?
B) Umm, yeah, it's called a knife.
C) I only buy Cheddar that is pre-grated.

Outdoor pursuits?
A) I have a special storage unit devoted to my hiking/camping/snow-trekking/wife-carrying activities.

B) The local park has a nice café.
C) If I can't find the remote
control, I might watch
a gardening program.

**How many umlauts are there
in your name?**
A) Two, and a slashed Ø.
B) TBH I never learned how to
type an umlaut on a computer,
so thankfully there are none.
C) Is this some kind of foreign
egg dish?

**How much do you care about
your carbon footprint?**
A) Enormously, I charge my
phone with energy powered by
a stationary bike set up in my
living room, and I haven't had
a hot shower since 2005.
B) I try not to take unnecessary flights,
so that's just summer, spring break,
Thanksgiving, Christmas...
C) If I buy my Doritos in the nearest shop,
does that count as local produce?

How beautiful are you and your family?
A) We've done the odd campaign for
Boden... Well, 17 to be specific; plus my
kids—Gunnar, Magnus, and Pernille—
all have a pair of H & M dungarees named
after them.
B) Are we talking with or without a filter?
C) I'm not even sure I want that picture of
my son on the wall.

Saunas—where do you stand?
A) I have one in the basement, but of
course I don't stand up in it. I lay. Naked.
B) There's one in my gym, I've tried to
sweat out the odd hangover in it.
C) Never been in one, but the extractor fan
in the bathroom has been bust for about
8 months. Does that count? Oh, that's
steam? Is that different?

*Mostly As: Congrats, you're totally a Nordic. Now
dash off for fika to celebrate.*
*Mostly Bs: You bought a sheepskin rug when Elle
Deco told you to, but your heart's not in it.*
*Mostly Cs: You probably think people from Denmark
are called Denmarkish (or Dutch).*

RESULTS:

IS H & M TRYING TO TAKE OVER THE WORLD?

H & M, Hennes, Hennes and Mauritz... Call the Swedish outfitters what you will, but it's pretty likely that even pre your Scandi-phase you shopped there a fair bit because everything was a bargain. However, did you realize that those sneaky Swedes have probably been creeping into your wardrobe unknowingly? H & M owns practically half your local shopping mall and high street now, with multiple brands falling under their chicly affordable (-ish—we're talking to you & Other Stories) umbrella. Here's the lowdown...

COS

What is it? A grown-up H & M that, with a squint, sells clothes that could pass for pieces costing five times the price. They sell some interesting "architectural" garments—think funnel-neck sweaters that'd need neck-ring stretching to wear and dresses with pockets in entirely impractical places. When trying things on, be prepared to ask yourself the following about everything: "Is this black or really dark navy?" It's nearly always black, FYI.

Signature piece: A black (of course) long-sleeved dress with a complicated hem that you could wear if you were either a slightly jazzy Amish lady or a high-powered architect in a firm that specializes in reimagining former public conveniences into charcuterie bars.

WEEKDAY

What is it? The new kid on the block, stores will be coming your way very soon. Think of Weekday as H & M for those who find H & M too cheerful. Androgyny rules here, with millennial pink the shade *du jour*, regardless of what you keep in your pants. Their denim and sportswear has more than a hint of "juvenile detention center" about it and should be worn with the accompanying youth-offender-posing-for-my-mugshot posture.

Signature piece: A pair of mom/dad jeans cut to flatter 0.1 percent of the population— those with muffin tops and cankles need not apply. Weekday flogs the kind of ugly chic that only the truly beautiful can get away with. If you're really gorgeous, add a pair of socks and sliders to your jeans.

CHEAP MONDAY

What is it? We don't wanna say this is hipster H & M, but yeah, that's it in a "we used the seeds to make milk" nutshell. Sitting firmly in the "quirky" camp, they started by making actually pretty excellent jeans and now enjoy jumping on the seasonal bandwagon of whatever print or object is big on Insta— see avocado-print romper suits or artistic-impression-of-body-part T-shirts.

Signature piece: A unisex white vest with ambiguous slogan, cut so low on the armpits it breaks the Insta nipple ban.

MONKI

What is it? Cool H & M. Sassy as hell (a Monki wearer would probably say sassy AF), Monki deals hard in the kind of cutesy man-repeller pieces that millennials can't get enough of. Heels are stompy, dresses are oversized, and underwear has more than a hint of toddler— pizza panties anyone?

Signature piece: Anything high waisted. The Monki customer hasn't seen her belly button since 2011.

& OTHER STORIES

What is it? H & M for when you've got a mortgage. Grown up, chic, and oh-so-stylish, hit 30 and you'll want everything in here. You just might not be able to afford it. Pussy-bow blouses and unusually colored cashmere ("I'm cashmere, I should be boring, but I'm camo colored, so I'm cool!") reign supreme, and if an item of clothing stays still for long enough, the designers will put a frill on it.

Signature piece: A cotton dress that costs four times what it would in H & M and you can't justify buying until you look closer and realize... It's got a bow round the neck! Just take my entire paycheck!

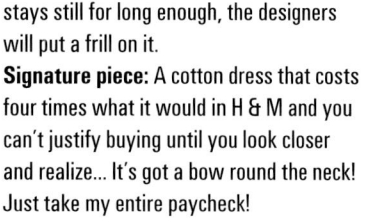

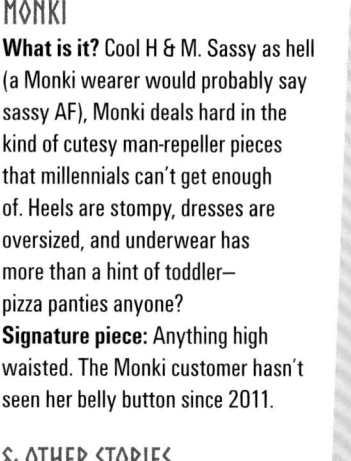

CANVAS BACKPACKS

When is a backpack not a backpack? When it's a $300 urban life accessory, of course. Scandi style might pretend to be all about chic minimalism, but there's one element that's in no way modest or pared back—the price tag. For the same price of one of these Emperor's new backpacks, you could book a flight to Reykjavík (or buy two beers when you're there).

THE FANTASY

You're picturing yourself cycling on your chicly ergonomic-yet-with-retro-stylish-design-features bike (this doesn't exist BTW Scandi wannabes, so relax before you burn off your fingerprints in your desperate googling attempts to buy one), your cropped black cigarette pants billowing slightly in the wind, your round tortoiseshell frames sitting perfectly atop your nose, and your unisex pea coat held perfectly in place by the jewel in the crown, your waxed canvas backpack.

The straps will sit just so, formed of tanned vegetable leather, or is it vegetable tanned leather? The former would suggest one could be wearing some kind of treated beetroot on one's back but hey, that'd be cool too. You're wearing the straps just baggy enough to suggest an air of Scandi insouciance (what do you mean "that's a French word, France is so not cool right now"?), but tight enough that they sit spirit-level straight. This style statement—you're not degrading it by calling it a bag—is functional too, holding everything you need to go about your fashionable day,

all while keeping your hands free for the important tasks of tucking your hair behind your eyes and readjusting the aforementioned tortoiseshell frames. Who could ask for more?

THE REALITY

Take a second look... Does the scene remind you of anything? History class maybe? WWII tin-hatted new recruits off to the frontline with their standard issue kitbags stuffed full of bromide-laced tea and pictures of their sweethearts. Yep, congratulations, you've just spent a week's rent on a glorified standard-issue army knapsack. Maybe your next step could be blowing a day's wages on a pair of socks made from half an unraveled child's sweater? Looks aside—'cos if there's anything being a Nord-chic slave has taught you, it's that purchases are about functionality too—the bag is also incredibly useless! It can be worn one of the following two ways, with both methods being completely impractical!

Option one: Stuffing your limited edition Sandqvist Sven-Goran bag to the gills,

so your cycling shoes/pilates Vibrams/ standard-issue US Army military fatigues strain against the fabric in the manner of a two-week-overdue baby's foot poking out of its mother's abdomen.

Option two: Use it to carry one single sheet of paper. TBH, you've been paperless since 2011, so that's not much use to you either. Realistically, you don't need to carry anything more than your phone and wallet with you all day and you keep those in your pocket anyway, because a roll-top canvas knapsack isn't exactly the most secure type of luggage.

MEN'S TURTLENECKS AND SNOODS

OK, we get the message: it's cold, necks are delicate things, and they need a gentle hug from some form of clothing. However, in Scandi-land it's not enough simply to zip your coat up right to the top or wear a scarf your grandmother knitted you for Christmas. Oh no, here adorning your neck isn't merely a way of avoiding hypothermia and/or hiding the razor cuts from the blade you should have changed two weeks ago, it's a way of life. However, male neckwear is a tricky look to pull off...

THE FANTASY

In the world of Nordic gentlemen's winter clothing there are two contenders vying for the title of "chicest neckwear." In the blue

corner we have the sporty, international-traveler approved, I-might-have-just-skied-here snood, or cowl as it's also known. It will be artfully slung around your neck, which is well tanned thanks to several winter-sports holidays, and the snood is just begging to be gently entwined around the delicate shoulders of your beautiful blonde female companion when she gets a little chilly. Worn with sunglasses just mirrored enough to provide you a little mystique, you think the overall effect of the snood will be to give you a ruggedly stylish appearance.

If the snood is a little too fey for your tastes, then let's head over to the opposing corner and say hello to the turtleneck. This item of knitwear must be worn tight enough to show those defined pecs that you'd like

to pretend were from chopping wood or commandeering a husky sleigh, but are in fact the result of an $80-an-hour personal trainer called Andi (we all know it should be a Y). You'll wear the sweater tucked into jeans for an artfully retro look that'll once again highlight the flatness of your stomach (thanks again Andi), while elongating your neck and showing the world in a subtle way that you're both couldn't-car-less manly and buff as anything.

THE REALITY

Let's talk snoods first. Maybe you don't even call it a snood; maybe you call it a cowl, or worse, an infinity scarf? Maybe you deserve to die by asphyxiation at the hands of the aforementioned "infinity scarf?" You know what that infinity scarf really says? It screams (particularly when worn by bald men), "look at me, don't I remind you of an uncircumcised penis!?"

From a practical point of view, taking a snood off or putting it back on is a gymnastic maneuver requiring an entire arm span of space. OK, yes, if you're doing winter sports it's handy not to have the trailing edges of a scarf fly behind in your

wake as you hurtle down a slope on tiny castors with a kite tied round your waist (that's a winter sport right, if not it soon will be). Except you're not skiing, there isn't any snow, and it's not even cold. You're waiting for a number 28 bus and when it arrives the most energetic thing you might have to do is go to the upper deck. Therefore, you can cope with just a normal scarf.

"OK, I'm not enough of an idiot to wear a snood," you think, "but my neck does sometimes get chilly, so a turtleneck is cool, right?" WRONG! The roll-neck sweater is universally creepy and will not make you look like Steve McQueen in *Bullit*, a suave Copenhagen-based existentialist philosopher, or the ruggedly handsome captain of an Icelandic fishing trawler. You will look like someone who might be called in for questioning over the crew you hung out with in the '70s. Or Steve Jobs. Wear the sweater too tight and everyone will think you came fourth in a reality show where your claim to fame was getting drunk and naked in a hot tub and you now make a living selling protein powder on Instagram. Wear the sweater too loose and it'll make you look like you've piled on so much weight that social workers are considering forklift removal to get you out of your bed.

Trust us, it's probably safest just to avoid these two items of clothing altogether Scandi-fans.

SCANDINAVIAN MUSIC

So you're pretty convinced that **EVERYTHING** about the Scandinavian countries is cool. You're on board with the fashion, the food, and the way of living (only you probably don't call it "way of living," you've probably adopted some natty Scandi phrase for that), but there might just be one facet of Nordic life that you haven't considered. Allow us to remind you of Scandinavian music.

"Yeah, whatever," you say, "There's loads of really hype electro actually, and have you checked out the space disco scene in Bergen? It's not all ABBA you know." And you'd be right, it isn't just ABBA; there is also A-ha, Ace of Base, Aqua, Alphabeat, and loads of equally uncool bands that don't begin with an A.

ACE OF BASE

You've probably written off this group as one-hit wonders thanks to their creepy "All That She Wants (Is Another Baby)," which everyone took a decade to realize was about having multiple boyfriends rather than a pro-life anthem about actual newborns. Actually, they had a few other hits too, enough to release a whole greatest hits album that included "The Sign," which sounded like it was recorded on a particularly bumpy bus journey while wearing uncomfortably tight pants, and, ummm, "Beautiful Life" and "Life Is a Flower." No, us neither.

A-HA

This Norwegian band is almost definitely responsible for every ill-advised one-night

stand that occurs at university. Ain't no hangover like an '80s-night hangover.

ALPHABEAT

The dance-pop churned out by these Danes was a total blessing for all TV producers who had never met a gay person. "Fascination" and "Boyfriend," which both sounded like they were created entirely from the limited selection of notes contained in the ringtone banks of a Nokia 3210, were at one point in the mid-2000s the only soundtracks any soap/murder mystery/police drama relied on to denote their scene was set in a "gay club." The band is probably still living off these royalties now.

AQUA

Rolling Stone magazine might have given the "so nasal they use it in ENT polyp-removal training seminars" "Barbie Girl" the title of worst song of the '90s, but we say "WHAT ABOUT 'DR JONES?'" It has the actual lyrics "Ah yippie yi yu! Ah yippie yi yeah! Ah yippie yi yu ah!" making up more than half the song; enough said.

AVICII

Swedish button presser (and before you jump in with "DJ, musician, and producer," may I in evidence give you the song "Hey Brother") Avicii is the worst, if for no other reason than he inspired the terrible song that starts "I took a pill in Ibiza, to show Avicii I was cool." Unless that pill was taken in a clinic in Switzerland and was

heralding imminent death, we're NOT INTERESTED MATE! From a collab with half-man, half-ketamine (keta-man?) David Guetta to the hideously hoedown-esque "Wake Me Up," it's hard to pinpoint which of his aural waterboarding anthems is the most painful.

BASSHUNTER

Between 2005 and 2008, this blond-haired (depending on his relationship with foiled highlights at the time), blue-eyed Hitler-Youth pinup was the litmus test for whether or not a nightclub was terrible. If you walked in the door and heard Basshunter's mom-techno anthem "Now You're Gone"—where he rhymes phone, strong, and gone—against a backdrop of illicit sticky-carpeted dancefloor foreplay, then you walked straight back out.

BJÖRK

Making a joke about someone whose greatest hit was "It's Oh So Quiet," when that's what 99 percent of the earth's population would prefer her to be, is too easy. So we won't.

THE CARDIGANS

If you remember a time when Leonardo DiCaprio wouldn't have won second place in a Jack Nicholson lookalike competition, then it's VERY likely you had one of your first sexual experiences to "Lovefool." The line "I don't care about anything, 'bout anything but you" may still have the power to make you tearful.

EUROPE

How many terrible New Year events have you attended where "The Final Countdown" was put on the stereo an optimistic ten minutes before midnight? Thus, how many fresh starts or moments to reflect on the passing year and your hopes and dreams for the future have been overshadowed by arguments about how many bars of "dur dur dur durrr, dur dur deh d'durrr" there are in the intro?

EUROVISION

In the Nordic countries, the Eurovision Song Contest* isn't a cheesy joke where a nation half-heartedly enters washed-up boy bands, those that came 13th in a Simon Cowell vanity project, and aging glamor models dressed head-to-toe in novelty condoms (if you're not from the UK, google "Katie Price Eurovision rubber" now). Scandinavians take the competition VERY seriously, and not even in an ironic "let's have a Eurovision party and dress up as ABBA and each come dressed as a different nation's flag and the LOLs we'll have if there are two Slovenias" way. Can you really commit to the lifestyle of a country that holds a national inquiry if it fails to qualify for the finals show or scores the dreaded "*nul points?*"

* For readers lucky enough to be unaware of Eurovision, think of it as an annual singing competition for the worst vocalists from *Insert you home country*'s Got Talent, pitted against the other worst acts from every other European country's version of the franchise.

REDNEX

Think of the hillbilly hideosity of "Cotton Eye Joe" as the forefather of Avicii's "Wake Me Up," laying down the roots to make novelty dance-country-and-western a legitimate music genre. Rumor has it that the whole song was about STDs, with "Cotton Eye Joe" referring to genital swabbing. One thing's for sure, the song has definitely never caused a sexually transmitted infection—can you imagine having sex to that racket? Unbelievably, Norwegians liked "Cotton Eye Joe" so much that it spent 15 weeks at the top of the charts, which surely caused a drop in birth rates the following year.

ROXETTE

You know what, we'll hand it to the Swedish duo, "It Must Have Been Love" is a pretty good song. Sure it's cheesy as hell and it definitely isn't fitting into your "current esthetic," but if you're going to get hammered and weep to a power ballad, there are a lot worse songs to choose. If we catch you strutting to "The Look" on the other hand...

SWEDISH HOUSE MAFIA

Electro house "supergroup" Swedish House Mafia are the favorite act of middle-aged investment bankers and grown-up "party girls" who should have left their cocaine days back in the '90s, mainly because these two factions were the only people who could afford to spend 100 euros on a ticket to watch the three DJs stand in front of generators on a hastily put-up stage and shout about people being "legends" at some pool party in Ibiza. For anyone else with ears, Swedish House Mafia's success was a total mystery. Or in fact anyone else with eyes, because, with a sleight of hand Houdini would be proud of, SHM used the proverbial smoke and mirrors (with added lasers) to trick you into forgetting they were just three leather-jacketed men who, in another lifetime, could have been presenters of *Top Gear Sweden*.

WHIGFIELD

With the very, very possible exception of "The Hustle"—purely for iconic status— songs that come with their own dances are generally A BAD THING. And the worst thing about Whigfield's "Saturday Night?" When you hear it at a wedding/40th birthday party/'90s' club night (why you'd go to the latter is a mystery), you become convinced you know all the steps, but you are bound to get your "jump back with hands crossing" move out of sync and whack Aunt Jean right in the chops.

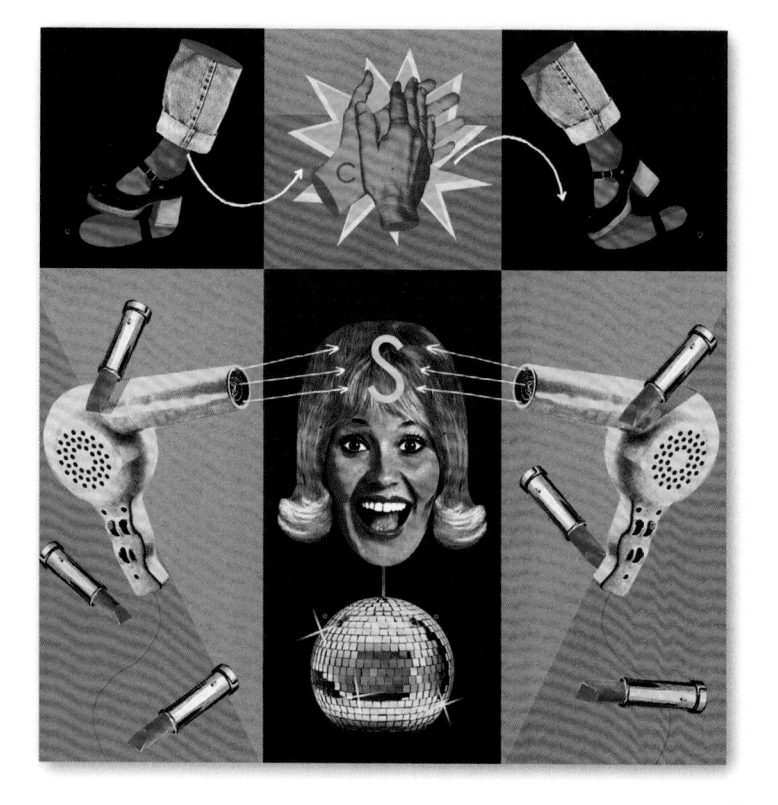

ICE-WHITE HAIR

As Hitchcock said: "Blondes make the best victims." The best victims of this epidemic of Scandi-wannabe hair-dyeing madness, that is. Bottle-blonde hair is big business and it's no longer OK for your locks to be vaguely golden or yellow, one's 'do can't even be buttery, creamy, or—heaven forbid—caramelly (why do top stylists insist on referring to hair color in calorie-laden dairy terms, especially when none of their clients have consumed any of the aforementioned since 1998?). When it comes to hair dye, "ice white" is the only acceptable shade if you really want to jump headfirst into full Scandi-ness. Sadly, achieving the look is not as simple as an agonizing four hours at the salon, sat under a mask of something that'll shift the limescale off your toilet in seconds. Consider what follows a friendly warning...

THE FANTASY

Your new hair color will make you look ethereal, other worldly, just like the one with the dragons off *Game of Thrones*. It'll be the perfect accessory for your chic, architectural, all-black wardrobe. The shade will make you stand out in a crowd and the only other adornment you need will be a minimal slash of red lipstick, which will become your "statement look." You'll constantly be asked to have your photo taken to feature on street-style websites, where the photos will show you looking wistfully away from the camera, your curtain of platinum shrouding your face in stylish mystery. One day, one of these street-style pictures will be used in a poorly researched article called "The ten most stylish women in Greenland" or "425 outfits that'll make you want to be a Danish girl, RIGHT NOW" and you'll be able to die happy.

THE REALITY

If your natural hair color registers anywhere below Simon Cowell's teeth on a dentist's "whiteness" score chart, but you still desire Scandi ice-white hair, then say hello to poverty and pain. And roots. No, not the kind of roots that require canal treatment, but, TBH, sorting out the roots in your mop can be just as agonizing. The first time you bleach your hair will be the worst. Actually, that's not true, but it's what you'll tell people because you can't lose face. And losing a bit of your face,

well, your scalp, is exactly what will happen. Don't believe us? Try googling peroxide scabs. Ouch.

Still want the ice-white hair? Well, be prepared for the haircut equivalent of five o'clock shadow, because no matter how close to your scalp the hairdresser gets, in approximately 2–5 days you'll see the first appearance of roots. These will initially crop up as tiny black dots that at first you might mistake for an insect infestation, but soon the little spots will jump from resembling ground pepper to Myra Hindley-esque, grubby-looking dark smudges that'll make your locks appear frying-pan greasy, no matter how many times you wash them. And, for goodness sake, don't wash it! Your mane has already been to hell and back and now even the merest confrontation with water, shampoo, or anything resembling heat styling (bleached hair has been known to suffer when in proximity to human breath— probably—so God knows what your Parlux hairdryer is gonna do to it), will cause it to admit defeat and shatter in your hands. Maybe just book yourself in for half a head of highlights then?

NORDIC ICONS

Name a famous person or character who comes from a Nordic country, but isn't in ABBA. Ha, knew you couldn't. No matter how many reindeer antler coat racks you're in possession of, it seems like your knowledge is pretty gappy. Here's your cheat sheet of the Nordics to know.

ALEXANDER SKARSGÅRD

When people wonder about the rise of Scandi tourism they cite many things: the culture, the food, the laidback way of life. This is all well and good, but what it's not taking into account is the Skarsgård factor. Around 65 percent* of all visitors to Nordic countries go there purely in the hope of licking a pair of Skarsgård-inspired cheekbones. Because everyone looks like that in Sweden, right? Tree height, pectoral muscles carved from rock, hair that sweeps back as dramatically as the curtain in a magician's disappearing act, a beard that you just know will scratch in only the right places... Sorry, not the case. The Viking genes do mean there are plenty of tall men, but also with the girth to match—all that reindeer steak and blubber-rich fish has gotta go somewhere. If pecs do exist, they are usually hidden under 17 layers of flannel. What about the beard? As with all facial hair, this will definitely have some of this afternoon's lunch in (blubber again probably). NO ONE actually looks like Alexander Skarsgård; not even Alexander Skarsgård. So if he's the reason for your EasyJet splurge and Stockholm city break, make sure you've at least got a backup plan.

*Statistic completely made up.

SARAH LUND

Hardy of skin (do you know what those jumpers feel like against your flesh? Itch central) and stern of face, Sarah Lund (AKA her off *The Killing*) is the woman that men who are frightened of their wives claim they fancy at dinner parties. "So unsexual, she's sexual," you say, confidentially hoping no one else around the table also read that line in *The Times* article about Nordic Noir. If you then go on to call her "the thinking-man's-crumpet," then quite frankly you deserve to be the victim of one of her next cases.

MADS MIKKELSEN

Creepier than some of Donald Trump's comments about his daughter, Ivanka, professional baddie who it's still OK to fancy a bit (but not too much), Mads Mikkelsen has built an entire movie career upon being able to convey all emotions through the medium of squinting. Sadness = three-quarter squint; malevolence = half squint; mid-murder = it's a wonder he can see anything at all. Mads is not just about semi-shut eyes though, oh no. There's also the matter of his trademark side-swept hair, last seen on Victoria Beckham circa 2002. So, he's a visually impaired, 15-year-old Spice Girl. Not quite so menacing now, hey Mads?

BJÖRN BORG

Whisper the words "terry-toweling headband" to women of a certain age and watch as they sink into a lust-fueled reverie for a few minutes, while memories take over of Björn Borg's sun-kissed pompadour/shorts so tight you could tell his religion. Nowadays, we might scoff at the fact that the tennis champ had the exact same hairdo as Camilla Parker Bowles and his style has become the default fancy-dress outfit for anyone wanting to lampoon '70s sportsmen, but back in the day a drop of sweat flicked from the aforementioned headband could cause grown women to faint.

HANS CHRISTIAN ANDERSEN

The Danish fairy-tale spinner has brought nothing but joy and pleasure to children's lives with his beautiful stories, right? WRONG. His fairy tales are creepy as hell. Take *The Little Mermaid*, in the Disney version it's all great hair, singing crabs, and happily ever after. However, in HCA's telling the mermaid only gets the leg/tail transfer for the price of being in constant agony as it feels like she's walking on knives. Then, because she isn't sweetness and light any more— walking on knives tends to do that to a person—the prince dumps her for someone else and the Little Mermaid kills herself.

You think that's bad? OK, let's look at a few more... In *The Princess and the Pea*, her royal highness is constantly waking up in bed bruised all over, the girl in *The Red Shoes* gets her feet chopped off with an axe (what have you got against women walking, buddy?), and the eponymous *Ice Maiden* is basically the grim reaper in snazzier clothes. Sleep well children...

LISBETH SALANDER

Stieg Larsson's unhappy take on the manic pixie dream girl, Lisbeth Salander is a manifestation of all our teenage emo selves. And she's probably responsible for more teenage goth boys changing their sheets than RedTube. Portrayed on film and TV in various different guises, Lisbeth's appearance veers from freshly out-of-a-BDSM-dungeon badass to hen-pecked starling—the discrepancies are, one suspects, dependent on each director's sexual peccadilloes. Larsson claimed she's Pippi Longstocking as an adult (more of her later), which does rather make us worry about what happened to poor Pippi in her teenage years. It's quite the jump from lugging one's horse about for larks to refashioning oneself as some kind of psychotic death-metal Robin Hood.

TROLL DOLLS

If you were a child of the '60s—and let's be honest if you're reading this book you probably aren't because chances are you picked it up in Urban Outfitters or similar and everyone knows you're not allowed in there post 32—or the '90s, when troll dolls made an unexplained return, then they were a big part of your life. Attached to anything and anyone that could host a small plastic, grimacing, *Something-About-Mary*-haired monster (in the '60s they sat atop pencils; '90s' trolls dangled from backpacks as "charms"), these Danish trinkets were a totally unexplainable fad. Nowadays relegated to the dashboard of people who refer to themselves as "kooky" and the bedrooms of adults who have probably never taken their underwear off in the presence of another person, there was a brief troll resurgence in 2016 with the hellish trip that was the movie *Trolls*. Thankfully, it's all gone quiet since then, but if you're still hankering after more, here are some "fun" troll facts for you...

- Trolls were originally made out of wood. Try carting one of those round swinging from the end of your Nokia 5210.

- In 1964, demand for trolls was so high that the manufacturers bought up Iceland's entire annual wool harvest in order to create the toy's signature hairstyle. Admittedly, we don't know how many sheep were in Iceland in 1964—there could have been, like, five—but it sounds impressive.

- In 2003, Florida used trolls to do police work. Yep, the cops bought 5,000 trolls, put them in police uniform, and handed the toys out to the general public in the hope it would make the police force appear more approachable. What the hell?! Isn't the point of the police that criminals are scared of them? A serial killer isn't exactly going to rethink his ways after being gifted a creepy little piece of plastic junk. In fact, it'll probably give him more ideas.

GRETA GARBO

Would it be trivial to reduce Greta Garbo, one of the greatest actresses of all time, to her eyebrows? Well, if you're this far into the book, we take it you probably won't mind too much. Like anorexic sperm daubed on a boiled egg, the two wispy strands sported by the Swedish-born actress were all the rage between the Wars. If you've got any nonagenarians to hand right now, you might find they're still sporting them. Aside from eyebrows, poor old GG also bears the dubious accolade of being the third-most popular person for idiots on Instagram to attribute quotes to* (ahead of Garbo are Einstein and Marilyn Monroe). The poor woman never even said her most famous line, "I want to be alone," but who cares when it looks so nice on your feed written in Cooper Black atop a deserted coastline?

*Again, statistic completely made up.

PIPPI LONGSTOCKING

You know what, maybe she was the blueprint for Lisbeth Salander. Actually, maybe Pippi's more evil. Why? Well, here's a warning to any parents trying to make a Pippi costume for World Book Day (which, judging by its irritating proliferation on Facebook, is an event that happens way more often than once a year): DO NOT put wire coat hangers in your child's hair to achieve Pippi's trademark right-angled pigtails. Over 53 people* were blinded last year by such fancy-dress carelessness. (And BTW, post-*Something About Mary* does anyone else find this gravity-defying hairstyle slightly creepy on a little kid?)

*You got it, we made this up too.

THOR

Imagine you were a Norse god. And not just any Old Norse god either, the god of thunder—that's basically the coolest, most badass god there is. Your wife's a fertility goddess and you're no slouch in the sexual stakes either. So far, so good. Now fast-forward to the 21st century and how are you being honored? Statues perhaps? Maybe some doctoral theses written about your every move? Cities named after you at least, right? Nope, nope, and nope. Instead we have Chris Hemsworth (not even the more interesting Hemsworth brother who is going out with Miley Cyrus) in a red bathrobe and a set of hair extensions a Playboy bunny might consider a bit tacky. Might be time to bring the rain down, hey Thor?

SCARLETT JOHANSSON

The bane of every celebrity journalist's life, Scarlett "is it two Ts or one and how many Ss and it's definitely a J not Y right?" Johansson (and yes we had to google the correct spelling) was admittedly born in New York, but with a Swedish great-grandpa, a Danish father, and a dual US and Danish passport, she's pretty authentic. Johansson is the archetype of what we think of as sexy Nordic women: perfect blonde hair (newsflash—the nearest that shade is to Scandinavian is its daily wash from a junior called Hans at her $800 a pop Fifth Avenue salon), healthily seductive curves from... Umm... Err... All that cow milking and butter churning (they do that over there, right? Or was that just a trippy dairy-themed entry into Eurovision one year?), and a complexion that screams, "I go outside a lot (but only with an SPF 50 sunscreen all over my face and, yes, oxygen facials totally count as outside, thank you very much)." Let's face it, looking like Scar-Jo (saves googling the spelling again) is rather more about dollars than Danishness.

YES OR NO-RDIC?

OK, OK, we just really wanted to get that pun in. In reality, this quiz is more "true or false," but you get the drift. How much—and there's not a single question in here that relates back to your "esthetic" we're afraid—do you really know about your favorite land masses?

1. They don't believe in Santa.
TRUE
This is not quite as mean as it sounds— Finnish adults don't go around whispering in the ear of toddlers, "he's not real FYI, you small idiot." Instead, they have Joulupukki, who's kind of the same thing, only he comes on Xmas eve. This might initially sound good to parents who'd like to avoid the 4am Christmas Day wakeup call, until they realize that when Joulupukki visits the kids have to meet him. This requires a parent to wear a convincing outfit to fool the kids, rather than them catching a glimpse of dad in a red beanie and a cottonwool beard when they're pretending to be asleep.

2. They put babies in boxes.
TRUE
"So far, so much meanness to kids," you're thinking. But you'd be wrong, because babies absolutely love hanging out in boxes. Actually, they don't really care, because they're babies. They don't even know they have a head, let alone have the wherewithal to start criticizing their sleeping arrangements. All babies in

Finland get given a welcome to the world kit from the goverment, which includes a box for them to sleep in. Of course, hipster companies have hijacked the idea and the boxes now come with hand-painted murals of gender-neutral play scenes and cost a small fortune, but the cardboard box your TV came in will do just as good a job. *

*Yeah, maybe not...

3. They love booze so much they have a special word for getting off their face at the weekend.
TRUE
Norwegians are passionate about their binge drinking; so much so that they have a wonderfully onomatopoeic (come on, it's not that long since you took English; it means a word that sounds like what it's describing, bees buzzing and all that?) word to describe it: *helgefylla*. That couldn't sound more like an excess of drink if it tried. "Drink a lot last night, bro?" you ask. "Yeah, a *helgefylla*." Perfect.

4. Finland and Iceland are not part of Scandinavia.
TRUE

No funnies this time kids, this information is purely educational. Technically, Scandinavia is only made up of Denmark, Norway, and Sweden. Don't panic though, because Iceland and Finland come under the branch of Nordic, so your Icelandic pendant lights and Finnish fold-up bike are still cool.

5. 80 percent of people in Iceland believe in trolls.
TRUE

And not even the kind of troll you find on Internet comments sections; we're talking full Billy Goat Gruff here. Icelandic roads are even planned to go around places the locals believe trolls are living in.

6. You get a pepper grinder as a consolation prize for being single.
TRUE

Danish and not married by 30? There's a handy condiment dispenser coming your way. Why? Get your minds out of the gutter, it's nothing to do with phalluses. Only it is a bit, because nowadays the tradition is to up the whole "oh, it looks a bit like a penis" aspect. Don't worry though, you don't have to wait 'til 30 to be single shamed. When you hit 25, Danes will chuck a lot of cinnamon at you if you don't have a ring on your finger. Presumably so people

want to come and... umm... lick it off you? Still, that probably beats a date with some of the weirdos on Tinder.

7. Speeding carries a bigger punishment than heroin possession.
TRUE

Those Norwegians really do not like fast cars—go 10 miles over the speed limit and it can be a $500 fine. Caught with a little bag of "H?" That's just $250-ish please. And in Sweden, if you're a good driver then you get put in a lottery where bad drivers fund the prize money.

8. A penguin is Colonel-in-Chief of the Norwegian Army.
TRUE

Brigadier Sir (yep, he's been knighted too) Nils Olav currently resides at Edinburgh Zoo in Scotland, where he presumably works remotely in his role as chief of the King of Norway's Guard.

THE 10 WORST THINGS ABOUT BEING A NORDIC

So you've got this far into the book and, despite our best efforts, you still remain unsold on the idea of giving up your Scandi obsession. OK, here's one more try—10 aspects of Nordic life that really are bad...

1. TAXES

All Nordic countries pay huge amounts of tax. Denmark pays the highest in the world, with the average Dane paying 45 percent in income tax. If you earn just 1.2 times more than the national average wage, the rate shoots up to 60 percent, which means you work until THURSDAY LUNCHTIME and the state gets every penny you earn. That leaves just one and a half day's worth of your wages in your pocket. You do sort of get it back in

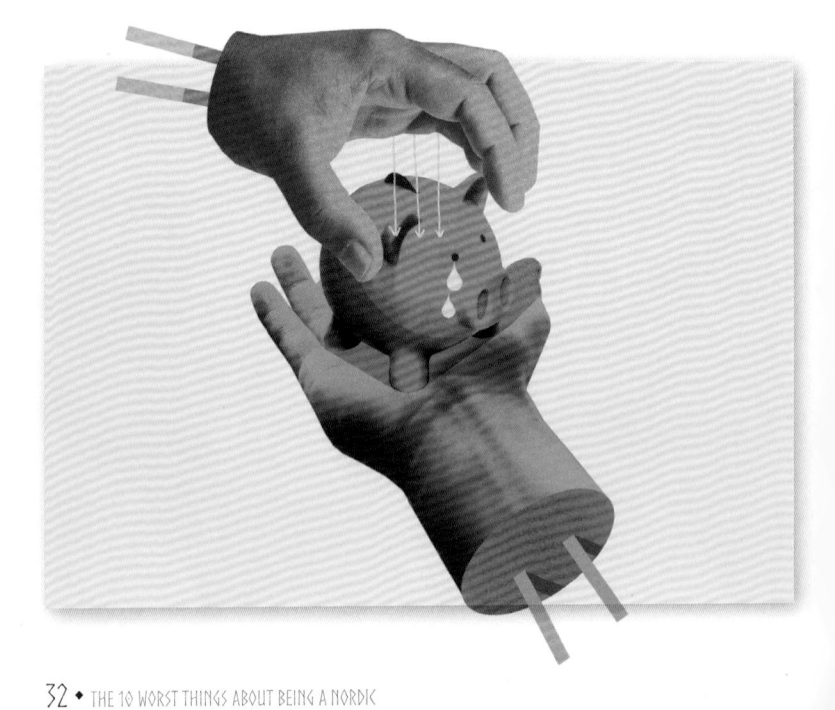

schools, old folk's homes, childcare, hospitals, and kindergartens, but you'll just have to pop out a sprog, get really old, or get ill to get any of it back.

2. WEATHER

Oh, it's so romantic and picturesque over there. Yes it is. It's perfect for your weekend minibreak, when you are escorted from taxi to Airbnb in your Uniqlo heat-tech layers and Canada Goose parka that you spent more on for these three days than you did on the whole holiday. You'll half-heartedly wear these clothes again when you have a cold snap at home, but you know in your heart that, unless you're nude under that coat, you're gonna be far too hot. The snow pics you take over the weekend barely need a filter on Insta and the novelty of breakfast, lunch, and quite possibly dinner all taking place in darkness is impossibly sexy. So far, so good.

Now imagine it's not three days in freezing-cold darkness, imagine it's six months since you had any vitamin D, and you've got the kind of seasonal affective disorder you'd need to install Las Vegas-esque levels of light therapy lamps to make a dent in. Not quite so much fun now is it?

3. PEOPLE BEING DISAPPOINTED WHEN YOU DON'T LOOK LIKE ALEXANDER SKARSGÅRD

If you're not at least six-feet tall and don't possess cheekbones that smaller species of birds could shelter from the rain under, but your name is still full of S's, then people are not going to be happy when you turn up to parties. "Ohmigod! Your friend Magnus Magnusson (no, not that one, RIP), he's Swedish, right? Can't wait to meet him... Oh, he's that short guy with jowls, hmmm, just going to grab a drink." Women: see Scarlett Johansson

4. NUDITY

Everyone likes saunas, yes? Well, for five minutes when you're in a fancy hotel and you really feel you must "experience all the facilities" 'cos the hotel was way over budget, but it did come with a spa so you're getting your damn money's worth. Or maybe when you've got a soaking swimsuit at the pool and you want to dry your butt quickly to stop your wet things stinking out your bag after you forget you put them there until next week. Hang on a minute, speaking of swimsuits, they're a no-no when you're Nordic. It's nude or nothing in a Finnish sauna as they consider swimwear at risk of giving off toxic fumes when heated (bet they've never tried to dry

a pair of wet underpants in the microwave either, or is that just us?) and with one sauna for every 1.8 people—yep, you read that right—they're as common in Finnish homes as upcycled driftwood tables. This means accept dinner invitations from anyone you don't want to see *sans* their kit with trepidation, because post your *grillimakkara* (to get this joke we're going to have to explain this is a Finnish sausage) you'll be getting your buns out too.

5. YOU MUST LIKE EUROVISION IN A NON-IRONIC WAY

No stupid drinking games where you down a shot every time someone does a rap in the middle verses. No shouting "it's all a fix" when neighboring countries give each other 12 points. You're in Scandinavia now, so you've got to take this stuff seriously. And watch the WHOLE THING. You're not even allowed on Twitter to read some of the sarcastic comments.

6. BOOZE

The problem here is two-fold. Firstly, alcohol is crazily expensive (see point 9); secondly, that doesn't hold many people back from glugging gallons of the stuff. It's considered bad form to leave a party when there's anything left in a bottle (so far, so good), but less good is the fact that binge drinking is a national hobby in most Nordic countries. Scandis put it away in volumes

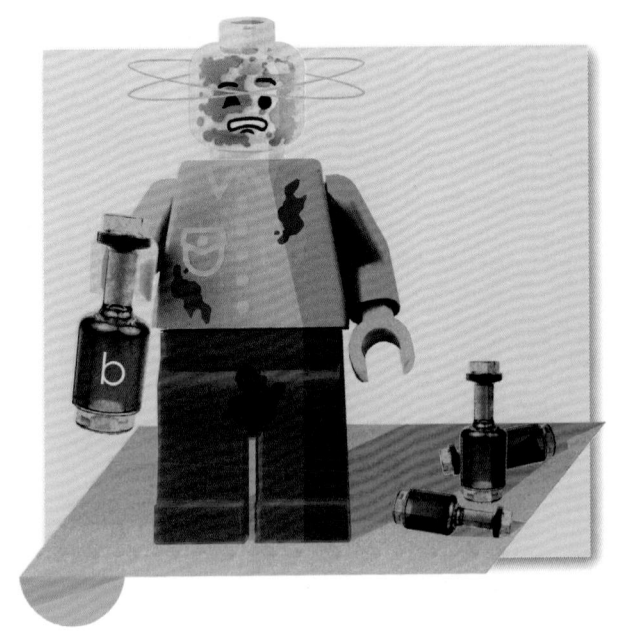

that make St Patrick's Day in Dublin look like a vicar's tea party. Alcohol-related illnesses are the leading cause of death for Finnish men and second for Finnish women. Apparently the love affair with getting hammered is all down to a "warrior" gene—those rosy cheeks you thought were from wholesome outdoor activities don't look quite so cozily pastoral now.

7. THE SWEDISH CHEF FROM THE MUPPETS

"Haha, say meatballs, I bet you sound just like the Swedish Chef."

"I'm Danish."

"Oh just say it, pleassseee!"

"OK. Fine. Meatballs."

"Hahahaha, you sound EXACTLY like him!"

"I've lived in the US since I was 18 months old."

So go approximately six out of every ten conversations with every new person you meet.

8. FIVE PERCENT OF DANISH MEN HAVE HAD SEX WITH AN ANIMAL

So says the *New York Post*. We've yet to see such an act with our own eyes (thank God), so we'll reserve a little judgment.

9. EVERYTHING IS REALLY, INCREDIBLY EXPENSIVE

Books cost a fortune (yep, even this one), meals out require a mortgage, and if it's an actual mortgage you're after then it'd better be a big one, because houses can be Hollywood A-lister levels of pricey.

10. TV (APART FROM THE THREE SHOWS YOU'VE SEEN ON NETFLIX) IS REALLY BAD

Yeah, those detective shows about knitted sweaters and troubled policemen learning to face their demons while investigating various murders are pretty cool, but that's it. There's nothing else on apart from cheaply bought in, badly subtitled English and American dramas that are 20 years out of date and the occasional depressing documentary about depleting herring stocks in the North Sea.

WEIRD NORDIC HOBBIES

You've sorted your wardrobe, your interior esthetic, your TV, your cuisine... What the hell is left? Well, those Nordics get quite a lot of downtime you know, so if you wanna emulate them properly you're going to have to get yourself some HOBBIES! Never mind that the last time you had a hobby that wasn't "scrolling through Instagram in bed 'til I lose feeling in my hand and drop my phone on my face" was when you were taught to do your CV at school and under "Hobbies and Interests" you put "socializing with friends and listening to music." If you want to go full Scandi, you might need to put some of these in your calendar.

BANDY

No, not a sport that involves walking like you've been on a horse all weekend (we wanted to say something ruder, but in the spirit of being Scandi and not sniggering at sex we won't), it's actually a winter team sport that involves hitting a ball with sticks on ice. So it's ice hockey then? Yeah, now you come to mention it... But seriously, there are some differences—the pitch is bigger and the ball is smaller! See, it's a totally different concept. It also doesn't make billions in TV revenue like its more glamorous brother, ice hockey. That's probably 'cos the teeny-tiny ball wouldn't show up on 70-inch US TV screens.

SAUNA ENDURANCE

Right, before we get into this can we ask a question? Why is there no word for a phobia of saunas? You've got one for being scared of beards (pogonophobia), buttons (koumpounophobia), and losing mobile phone reception (nomophobia), but there's no word for the terror that comes when that door shuts, locking you into an inferno of hell that could actually kill you? The World Sauna Championships were held in Finland from 1999 to 2010, where competitors would sit in 110-degree heat (yep, that's 10 degrees hotter than the boiling point of water) for as long as they could tolerate. At the last championships in 2010, one finalist sadly died and another was seriously injured, meaning an end to this event. So for any potential sauna masochists reading, we're very sorry to have gotten your hopes up, but unfortunately you're going to have to give this one a miss.

PHONE THROWING

A "sport" (who decides this anyway?) since 2000, this surprisingly wasn't just a marketing ploy from Nokia to try to get people to find a use for their phones in a post-Apple world. No, phone chucking has rules and everything. Scores are based on distance traveled, technique, and there's a freestyle category where you get marks for choreography (we're imagining dressage with a handset?). There are even world records! Somebody tell Naomi Campbell immediately...

WIFE CARRYING

Originating in Finland, this involves chucking your better half over your shoulders—bottom against back of head and legs as handles seems to be the most popular hold—and then dashing up and down some hills and log hurdles. Why, you might ask? Why indeed. Apparently, it's something to do with folklore stories from back in the day of thieves making off with local women and dashing through the woods with them. You'd think it would make sense to pick the teeniest "wife" possible (we don't imagine you have to show a marriage license to enter nowadays), but as the prize is the aforementioned "wife's" weight in beer, it's a tough decision to make.

SCANDI-PHILE CHECKLIST: THE FIVE PRODUCTS ONLY THE DEDICATED WILL OWN

Sure, you're trying to learn Norwegian on the Duolingo language app and you now only wear comfortable shoes made by Ecco—the ultimate footwear brand for telling the world you've hit middle age—but how much have you REALLY integrated the Nordic way of life into your everyday comings and goings? Do you always go Scandinavian, even when the non-Nordic option would be way more palatable? Give yourself a point for every one of the following items you use at least once a day.

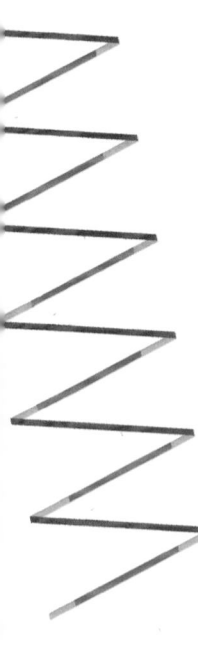

1. A VOLVO

This shows real commitment, because, despite the very best efforts of their marketing team and the astonishing paycheck Barbara Broccoli must have taken home for putting Daniel Craig in one in *Quantum of Solace*, Volvos are still the auto equivalent of the nice, reliable boy at school that your parents always wished you'd bring home for dinner. Safer than a bodyguarded bunker, it's a vehicle that says "they might as well have built in the child car seats."

2. A NOKIA PHONE

Once the king of the castle, Nokia is now very much the dirty rascal looking up at the turrets and wondering why it didn't shift its backside into updated tech a little quicker. If you're still using a Nokia post-2015 and you're not over 70, then we can tell you this now: YOUR FRIENDS HATE YOU! This is because a) you'll never have a charger they can use, and b) you're probably the kind of hipster that also refuses to listen to anything that isn't vinyl (despite not even being old enough to remember minidiscs).

3. A (SONY)ERICSSON PHONE

This one's for the slightly less committed Scandi-phile, as Sony stepped in to make the tech a little more palatable. Once up there with Nokia as the producers of the most lusted over phones, this Stockholm-based brand's fall from grace was quicker than a Koenigsegg Swedish supercar.

4. AN IKEA MALM BED (SEE ALSO: EKTORP SOFA AND LACK COFFEE TABLE)

Are you excited about the prospect of awarding yourself triple points for completing the Scandi hat-trick and owning all three of these IKEA bestsellers? Well congrats, that one second of time in which you got to feel thrilled is probably the greatest pleasure those objects are ever gonna give you. Sure, the Malm was fine in college where the popped-out bed slats served as trophies for your sexual prowess, and the changeable covers of the Ektorp were hella useful when someone couldn't quite cope during a keg challenge, but you're 45 now and you really should have invested in something more comfortable.

5. SKYPE

OK, not strictly a product, but if you still rely on Skype—founded by a Dane and a Swede Scandi-tag team—for your video calls rather than doing what the rest of the world does and use FaceTime, then you're very possibly either doing something you shouldn't or you're wedded to your PC due to point b) in the Nokia entry.

CALLING BS ON HYGGE

No one really knows how to pronounce it (Huggah? Hugg-e? Hi-gah? Higgy?), and no one really knows what it is. Perhaps it's something to do with candles and slippers and taking photos of your hot chocolate while you burn your hand because you're holding it uncomfortably over your faux-fur throw to get the perfect Insta picture? Maybe hygge was invented because living-your-normal-life-in-a-reasonably-cold-country-during-winter doesn't sound quite as catchy and wouldn't sell quite so much dross. This Danish lifestyle trend has a lot to answer for. Attached to everything from maxi pads* to front doors (heaven forbid one should have a non-cozy doorknocker— if you are committing such a crime, replace your doorbell with one that plays soft musical interpretations of dying fire embers immediately), we're still none the wiser as to what hygge actually means.

According to the countless identikit think pieces you can find online about hygge, the word means more than just cozy; more than "CBA to go out 'cos it's freezing and I'm skint;" more than "oh, this seems like a great way to add 20 percent onto the price of everyday garbage people already have/don't really need. Those in the know (ie no one, because it's not a real thing) claim hygge is indefinable, that it represents a sense of togetherness and a way to make ordinary moments more special. It's as yet unclear as to whether togetherness applies to being together with actual humans or just bonding with your cashmere-mix booties and whisper-of-child's-breath candle because you've lost all your real friends thanks to your obsession with a fictional lifestyle.

A quick flick through "#hygge" on Instagram and the hashtag covers everything from tattoos (not sure how the repeated jabbing of a needle into one's body adds up to cozy contentment) to engagement rings (can one snuggle up with a diamond?), alongside a large proliferation of bicycles leaning against walls (hey, if nothing else at least criminals are going to benefit from this because bike locks are distinctly un-hygge). Still, some items are definitely more hygge than others, especially when it comes to your home, or homeygge as some idiots are probably call it. How many of these have you been conned into buying?

* Probably, and if not yet 'tis only a matter of time. After all ladies, a normal menstrual cycle is sooooo un-hygge. You've got to upgrade your protection to a feel-good, treat-yourself product with a fresh pinecone deodorizer and faux-fur softness. Let's hope those two don't get mixed up, a pinecone texture in your underpants would not be pleasant.

1. SCENTED CANDLES THAT COST MORE THAN A MONTH'S GAS BILL

Remember when you only had one or two candles knocking around—the sickly sweet vanilla one you got from Kate in accounts for secret Santa that's gathering dust on a bathroom shelf, and/or the mandatory 40-pack of IKEA tealights (has anyone ever visited an IKEA and not bought them) primed for your next bedroom seduction. Nowadays, if you haven't got a curated collection featuring soy wax candles, scented with extract of 100-day-old lavender fused with Parisian morning dew, laid out carefully on a specially purchased candle display plate, then frankly you're lucky to still be part of society at all. Never mind the fact that constantly burning candles can give off potentially dangerous levels of formaldehyde or give you migraines or blacken your artfully painted ceilings (more on this later), they'll definitely get you double-figure likes on Insta.

2. FAUX FUR EVERYTHING

Rugs, cushions, pillows, throws, curtains (if they haven't happened yet, they will soon), for a truly hygge home it seems the aim is to give the impression that one is in the midst of a rather too close for comfort bear hug. Swaddled over sofas, "accenting" beds, and cozying up your kitchen, there's nowhere in your home that won't benefit from a touch of touchable chic. Apart from there is. The polar fur on the couch soon gets covered in coffee or tomato soup and is also too warm unless you open all the windows during a winter cold snap, the pillows on the bed shed all over the sheets and make you sneeze, and once you've walked on the Swedish rug in anything but sateen slippers it starts to resemble a mangy German Shepherd.

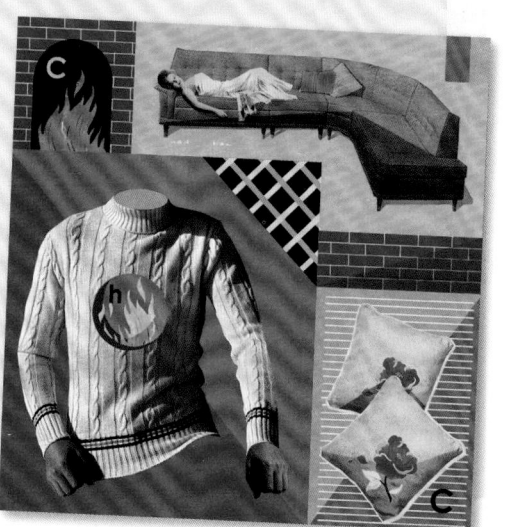

3. FLOOR CUSHIONS

When is a cushion not a cushion? When it's pretending to be a seat of course. Once upon a time, if you didn't have enough chairs for your guests to sit on you'd chuck them the cushions from the sofa. That gesture would stop your visitors getting piles from sitting on the cold floor, but would do nothing to diminish the guilt felt thanks to the fact you were still living like a student at 35. Now all you have to do is make sure the cushions are a little larger—and a lot more expensive—and they're a perfectly legitimate seating option. Be prepared for your mother to pick the cushions up every time she comes round though.

4. PILES OF CHOPPED WOOD

Wood artfully positioned in every available corner, placed nonchalantly on shelves, stacked in neat formations by doors... WHEN YOU DON'T EVEN HAVE A FIRE! What is wrong with you?

5. BASKETS

Anything that's not nailed down can be given the hygge treatment by chucking it into a lovely jute basket—toilet rolls, extra throws (throws are the hygge version of the Princess and the Pea and her 20 mattresses), lotions and potions... Hell, even other baskets. In fact, just put everything you own in ever-increasing baskets until your whole home is just one massive basket. That's what hygge wants.

NORDIC FOOD: SOME QUESTIONS

When it comes to eating Scandi-style, it's not all René-Redzepi-inspired New Nordic Cuisine or IKEA meatballs (delicious, no matter what anyone says). Thankfully, there's a whole lot more to Scandinavian food, but sadly not all of it is as palatable as your cinnamon buns and lingonberry jam (more of that later). Here are the burning (yes, pun intended) questions we have about Nordic food.

What the hell is a cloudberry?

No, it's not the matted back end of a sheep that a farmer needs to trim (that's a dingleberry, FYI), nor is it some annoyingly hipster shade of hair dye that you pay a small fortune for in a salon that ironically serves cans of Red Stripe (TBH it's probably this too, and is on their "unicorn hair" menu). According to Wikipedia, a cloudberry is in fact "a rhizomatous (nope, us neither—to save you googling, it's something complicated with roots) herb native to cool temperate, alpine, arctic tundra and boreal forest, producing amber-colored edible fruit similar to the raspberry or blackberry." Oh, of course! Why didn't you just say that? And you can buy the jam in IKEA.

And what's a lingonberry?

These are basically cranberries.

Are body cookies some kind of depraved sex act?

To be honest, all but the most puritanically minded of folk (although, come to think of it, they're often the worst) are going to see the term "body cookie" and have a terrible flashback to 2 Girls 1 Cup (if you don't know what we're talking about, DO NOT GOOGLE IT). But panic not, it's nothing to do with that. It also has nothing to do with the more offensive (in some people's eyes—and noses) products you can buy in Lush cosmetics stores*—if they don't have a cutesy rum 'n' raisin, pecan, mocha-choca shower body cookie on the shelves yet, it's only a matter of time. Instead, body cookies—known locally in Sweden as *kroppkakor*—are the actually quite innocuous sounding dish of potato dumplings filled with pork.

* FYI, if you're the CEO of Lush and this has given you an idea, we'd like a cut.

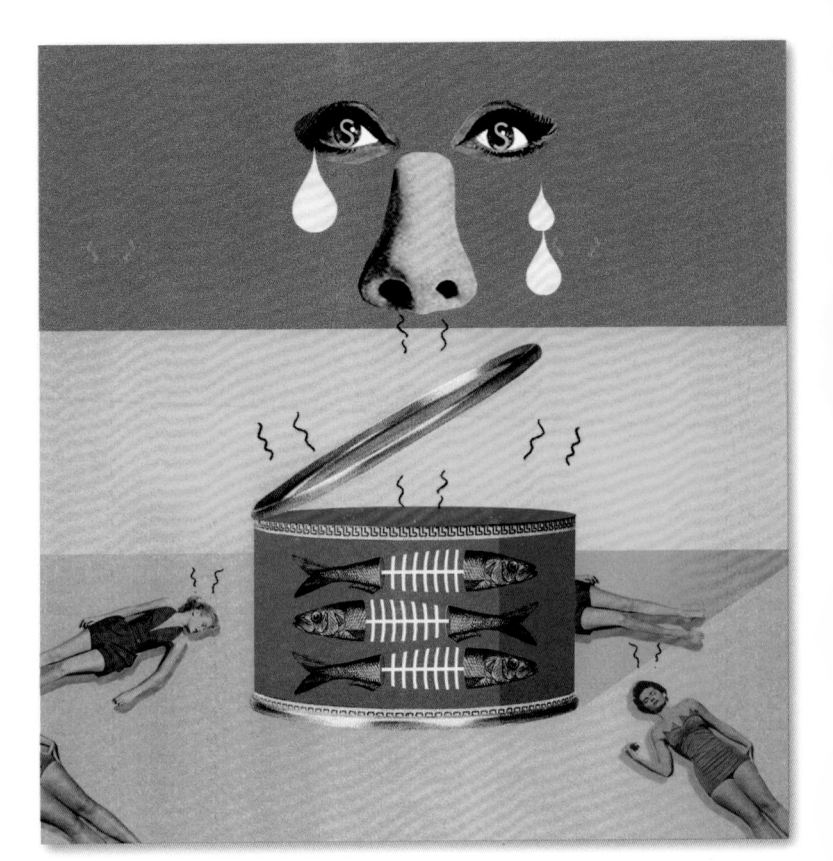

Can *surströmming* make you ill?
The EU has tried to ban it and the stench from an opened can has been known to cause people to vomit... Welcome to the wonderfully disgusting world of *surströmming*, AKA rotten herring. Yep, call it fermented, call it aged, dress it up however you want, but basically if you leave a formerly living thing for long enough, what does it do? IT DECOMPOSES!

Traditionally "enjoyed" (is that definitely the right word?) in Sweden at the end of summer, this canned "delicacy" is frequently removed from in-flight luggage because the risk of explosion from the build-up of gases caused by all the bacteria (ewww) is too great. A can is usually opened outdoors, because removing the lid in your home would result in a stench too foul to live with. Tenants have been evicted for committing the crime of chowing down on some *surströmming* within their four rented walls.

Tucking into these rotting fish is now a popular YouTube challenge (aka bequiffed men in their 20s pretending to be 15 by taking on "hilarious" tasks). The frequency with which "VOMIT WARNING" appears on these video descriptions would confirm that yes, *surströmming* can indeed make you sick.

See also: *hákarl*–Iceland's putrefied shark-meat delicacy.

Is drinking sour milk really a thing?
Of course not, silly. You might be thinking of the Swedish breakfast treat, *filmjölk*, which has a totally cool-sounding name that totally negates the fact it's, well, thick sour milk. Calm down though, so is yogurt. Kind of.

Ammonium chloride sounds like a bad thing. Why add it to candy and sweets?
It might sound worryingly like a chemical compound that causes severe allergic reactions in women who didn't do a patch test before dyeing their hair with that box of Nomorerootz; or something Walter White would've had to travel to six Home Depot stores to buy enough of covertly, but ammonium chloride is in fact a kind of acidic salt (calm down science nerds, that's as deep as we're going). For some strange reason, lots of Nordic countries add ammonium chloride to the

manufacturing process of licorice, turning what is already arguably the worst sweet treat on the shelf to something akin to a sheep's salt lick.

Is it true that Rachel Green's trifle in that *Friends* episode originated in a Scandinavian country?
Umm, not exactly. That might be something we made up for a cheap laugh, but when we explain to you what a Flying Jacob is you'll understand why. It's a dish of chicken, chili sauce, peanuts, bacon, and bananas, so basically a chicken and banana casserole. Swedes call *Flygande Jakob* the perfect midweek supper. We call them liars.

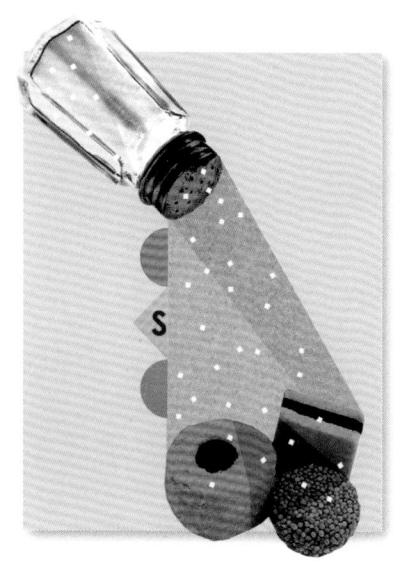

THE CASE
AGAINST LAGOM

Dear members of the media, we know that you're hungry for the next hygge. We know that lagom, the latest Scandi buzzword, is a horribly tempting candidate, given that it's easy enough to say and to spell, with no horrid umlauts for you to struggle to type on your keypad. Lagom also doesn't contain too many letters, so it's ideal for enticing article headlines and there's just enough confusion over how to pronounce it to make you feel superior at parties when you're the one to explain it correctly ("la" as in car and "gom" as it bomb, FYI). Plus, it has a vague enough English translation that means you can bend lagom to fit in with whatever subject you want to talk about. So far, so good, right? NO!

Unlike hygge, which—despite everyone claiming it's way more nuanced—basically boils down to being a lazy sofa-bound slob with slightly more expensive pillows (so actually a pretty nice way of living then), lagom is the opposite. So what the hell is it? The translation *du jour* of lagom is "just enough," and the *Elle Decos* of this world may try to fool you that "just enough" is a good thing. They say that it means sharing, simplicity, pared-back style and minimalism, finding out what's really important... Hmmm. Unpick the *Elle Deco* spin and what does "just enough" really mean? We'll tell you what: not as much as you'd like. Are you still in love with your wife? Just enough. Do you believe life is still worth living? Just enough. Did you enjoy your saved-up-for-all-year vacation?

Just enough. Doesn't sound quite so impressive now, does it?

Instead, think of lagom like a form of monastic abstinence; a sort of "oh, let's not bother making this any nicer" attitude. It's like discovering there's no free bar at a wedding or going to a friend's house for dinner and being given a plate of toast. Lagom is basically getting a birthday present of some homemade jam (probably vile cloudberry jam at that), which is completely unfair since it was all about hygge when it was your friend's birthday and you got them cashmere slippers! Or maybe lagom is a retelling of Goldilocks, but shut it blondie, because our version of too much is not the same as your version of too much and we'd have eaten all three bowls of porridge TBH.

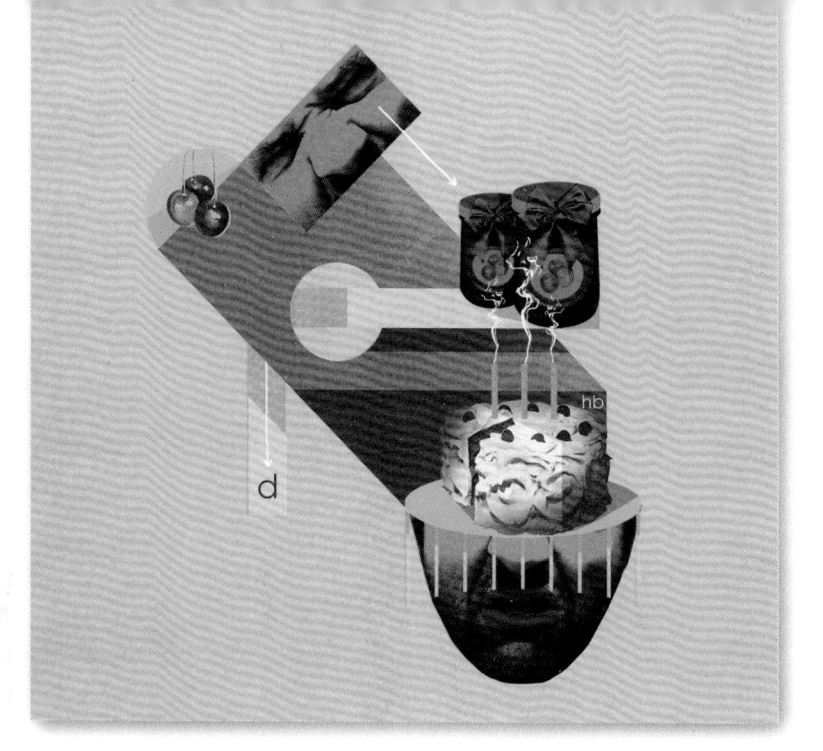

Of course, like hygge, lagom is really nothing new, just an everyday concept (don't overindulge, in this case) repackaged with a few hard-to-pronounce vowels. The British upper classes have believed in this way of life for years—living with a leaking roof and bedsprings that all but perform an appendectomy every time you roll over is as much a marker of class as having a family crest you didn't download from the Internet.

IKEA even set up a "Live Lagom" campaign. Of course they did, because anyone that's got too much isn't going to spend six hours on a public holiday pushing a wonky trolley around a gridlocked, artificially lit hell hole, mindlessly filling their bags with cut-price tealights and art prints as generic as a Big Mac. IKEA claim lagom is changing people's lives. For the worst, one imagines.

Apparently, hygge is about blissful moments, whereas lagom is more about getting on with your day-to-day business. Does this mean we can't lagom in cashmere, or will this create a terrifying lagom/hygge double-headed monstrous hybrid lifestyle that will turn on us all and cause us to self-combust with smugness? It's our responsibility to find out...

SEVEN SCANDI-INSPIRED INTERIOR DECISIONS YOU'VE PROBABLY MADE AND WHY THEY WERE A MISTAKE

Open up any Sunday supplement, walk into any home store, or look on any interiors website and you're bound to come across an article extolling the virtues of some Scandinavian home trend or other. Here are a few you can't have failed to miss...

1. WHITE FLOORBOARDS

They cost a fortune to sand, file, exfoliate, and whatever other treatment that cowboy artisan floorboard master craftsman claimed was necessary, but those white floorboards looked fantastic. For about two weeks, until that dropped glass of red wine made them appear more murder scene than minimalist chic. Next, that trodden-in dab of Nutella gave the floor more than an air of dirty protest. Come to think of it, the old carpet was also much cozier, easier to vacuum, and you didn't run the risk of splinters in your toes (sanded it did you Mr Artisan?). You should probably consider buying a large rug.

2. PENDANT LIGHTING

AKA the reason Steve had to have seven stitches in his eyebrow last time he came over, but it was his fault anyway for being too tall. And he was not looking where he was going—it's a light for God's sake, it should get noticed. Ceiling lights are strictly non-Scandi, so if your light source doesn't hang at decapitation-of-an-average-man height then it's not worth bothering with. Cracking the skulls of you and yours since 2015 and making your living space resemble a restaurant's plating-up area with overhead heat lamps, pendant lights are for some reason the second-most popular Nordic way to illuminate one's home. The first? Of course it's candles. Have you been paying attention to anything we've said so far?

3. FAUX ANTLER EVERYTHING

It started with antler coat hooks, which were kind of cool at the time. Plus, you were a bit bored of the metal ones you'd had since college that you slung over the back of a door, which meant it would never shut properly. Admittedly, you couldn't really hang much on the new antler hooks, but that wasn't really the point. As soon as any guests arrived and you took their outdoor garments (you'd already cleared

the two coats the hook could realistically hold and chucked them on your bed), these "antlers" announced that you were embracing Scandi cool. Therefore, the minor inconvenience of the coat hooks not actually doing the job they were designed for didn't really bother you.

From coat hooks you graduated to a faux hunting trophy that looked like the head of some be-horned creature. You think it was a reindeer, but it might have been a gnu (you're not actually sure what a gnu is), reimagined in some snazzy Scandi-folk-art print or the like. This served zero function other than to catch the shoulder of anyone

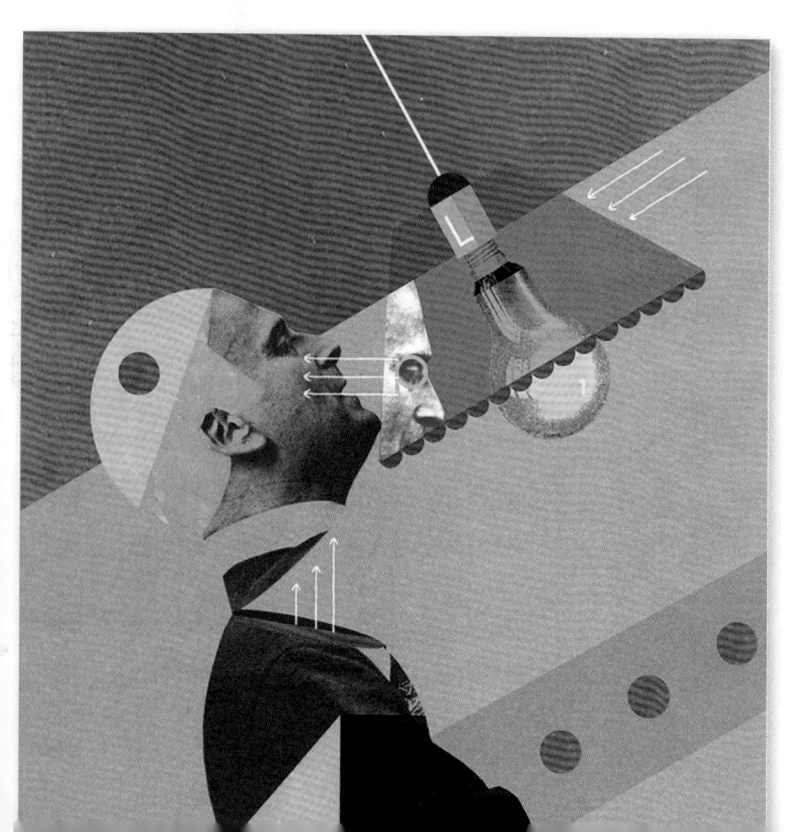

taller than 5 foot 11 who walked past it, and the head eventually fell prey to death by scented candle when someone lit one of your Diptyques too close to the antlers.

4. SHEEPSKIN OVER CHAIRS

One for the more discerning Scandi-phile, who sees straight through fake fur for the gimmicky marketing ploy it really is and heads instead for an authentic sheepskin every time. So what that it smells a bit mint saucy for the first six months? Draped over anything that stands still long enough (watch out Fido), an artfully thrown sheepskin rug can look great, but it might render some of your seats unsittable. Have you tried getting comfortable on a kitchen stool atop which sits a slippery half sheep? Perilous at the best of times.

5. COPPER EVERYTHING

Remember when all you saw of copper was if you hadn't finished decorating your bathroom properly and some of the pipes were still exposed? Not any more. Now everything from your toilet-roll holder to your coffee table is coated in the stuff. Copper, rose gold's grown-up sister, is a nightmare to stop looking tatty and shows up fingerprints better than a full forensic sweep, but any serious Scandi-philes won't let the impracticalities of hours of weekly cleaning put them off.

6. CACTI

You're congratulating yourself on not being a cliché and going for succulents over a cactus. Well, kudos to you; you're even worse. We bet your cactus is the only flash of color in a monochrome bathroom where you've decanted everything into black and white vessels. (FYI, we know it's Oil of Olay in that Aesop bottle.)

7. A TROLLEY DASH IN FLYING TIGER

This is the bargain-basement store you don't have to feel dirty about. Spend half an hour in Danish-born Tiger (or Flying Tiger as it's been rebranded) and, for less than the Uber you'll need to get home 'cos you've bought so much junk, you'll have enough nicknacks to cover every surface in your house. And then some. Take a look at the checklist opposite to see how you did on your shopping trip.

HOW MANY OF THESE CAN YOU TICK OFF?

☐ **Any kind of animal-shaped lighting**
A fluorescent bunny, we bet?

☐ **Some "comedy" stationery for your office**
A pencil sharpener that's a cat's backside? A stapler that's in the shape of a hedgehog? A USB-pluggable tea warmer that looks like a cake? The office ROFLs will never end!

☐ **Moustache-motif miscellany**
A mirror with a 'stache on? Hilarious placards you can hold up during a selfie to make you look as if you're sporting whiskers? Cushions in the shape of upper-lip hair? Hahahahahahaha!

☐ **Non-functioning cleaning equipment**
Shoes that are also mops! A bathroom trash can only big enough for disposal of cotton buds! Washing-up sponges in the shape of fruits!

☐ **Novelty bunting**
That you'll put up for New Year's/a birthday/the last episode of your fave Netflix original and will stay up until the day you move out.

☐ **Glassware that is so cheap you literally throw it around at parties**
This set of neon ice-cream-cone-shaped wine tumblers? A set of four that's less than the cheapest, foulest bottle of paint-stripper wine? Smash! Crash! It doesn't matter!

SEX: WHAT'S THE DEAL?

A genetically blessed population plus a cultural fondness of nudity SHOULD make for awesome sex, right? Add to that world-famous levels of sex education, unparalleled levels of tolerance and acceptance, plus a laid-back attitude to the comings (we won't make a joke here, it wouldn't be very Scandi of us) and goings of the body, and yes, Scandi sex look pretty appealing. It's not all après-sauna all-day sessions in a log cabin though (only it kind of is). Here are six reasons why Scandi sex is overrated.

1. RATIO-NO

Currently, there are a lot more men than women in Sweden—something like 108 men to every 100 women (you do the math). Although hang on, that is kind of a global trend too. Oh whatever, it's not easy thinking of negatives for a plethora of Swedish guys, you know.

2. BLONDES HAVE MORE FUN?

What if you can't bear a blonde? If tall, dark, and handsome is your type, then you might have to look elsewhere. Only you won't really, because, you know, hair dye exists and there's the mixing of gene pools.

3. IT'S COLD

Yes! A bona fide reason sex is better outside of Scandinavia. It's goddamn freezing and who feels like kicking off their PJs when it's ten degrees below? This also means that you might not get a chance to fully appraise your potential sex partner ahead of the act. Who knows what could be lurking under those three coats?

4. IT'S DARK

Obviously you'd be entitled to think that, yes, the fact it's dark means it's more fun to stay in and, you know... BUT maybe you're a person who likes "doing it" in natural light. If you need vitamin D to get your "D," then you're gonna struggle in 24 hours of darkness.

5. YOU MIGHT BE RELATED

In small towns with smaller populations, you never know who might be your second cousin once removed. As such, Icelanders have developed an app to tell you if you share DNA, before you, ahem, share DNA. "But what if my distant relative is really, really hot?" you ask. We guess it depends on how many fingers you'd like your future offspring to have.

6. NO AURAL SEX

Making too much noise doing anything is a no-no in Sweden (apart from when making bad music, see page 18), so if you're fond of a screamer, your luck might be out here.

THE DOWNSIDE OF NORDIC NOIR TV

Bringing down your mood since 2007, the furrowed brows, edgy fringes, bleak landscapes, and bleaker lives of the Nordic Noir drama has become our number one televisual mental health self-harm. Leaving your living room with a darkness like no other (in more than one way, see below for more details), we just can't get enough of the depressing monotony of policemen and women with failing health and a litany of emotional problems attempting to work out who killed Professor Hoeg in the sauna with a reindeer pelt... Here's why you must cut down on your NN habit.

MISERY

As a subject, murder isn't admittedly the most lighthearted, but hasn't anyone involved in any of these shows ever seen *Murder She Wrote* or *Poirot*? Hell, even a *Miss Marple* episode? You can inject a little LOL into all the misery, you know—those iced-over lakes and snow drifts are crying out for a couple of comedy pratfalls. And don't tell us there couldn't be a hilarious mix up over washing some Fair Isle at the wrong temperature?

SUBTITLES

OK, it's not exactly cool to admit it, but subtitles are one big enormous pain and anyone who pretends they're not is a liar. The only time subtitles are welcome is when you're at your gran's house and it's either read the text or risk your own hearing loss thanks to the extreme decibel level granny needs to follow the plot and/or the screeching from interference with her hearing aid. If you wanted to read a book, you'd read a book, and in these times of double screening, where we're definitely looking up what that girl's been in before/where we can get a shirt like that/what someone intelligent on Twitter thinks of the show so we can pass that off as our own opinion, anything that demands full attention feels too much like hard work. Missing a key plot development just 'cos you've had a push notification about "buy

one get one free" from Dominos isn't the only problem, subtitles are also hard to read when hungover or watching on a small screen—basically all of life—and you can't even run for a quick pee, leaving the door open to hear what's going on. Just us?

TOO DARK

Admit it, the first time you watched a Nordic Noir you fiddled with the contrast settings on your TV remote didn't you.

In fact, you probably didn't even know what contrast settings were before you gave *The Killing* a go and pressed every available button trying to figure out why everything was a shade of muddy green and gray. You're already squinting because of the relentless subtitles, so the fact 99 percent of these dramas look like they've been filmed in night vision really isn't going to do your eyesight any favors.

SCANDI THINGS THERE'S NO POINT IN TRYING TO GET AWAY WITH IRL

Yes, you can buy all of your wardrobe from Cos (see page 12), you can decorate your inner-city studio apartment in the manner of a turn-of-the-century-woodsman's cabin, you can send yourself semi-blind watching nothing but subtitled Scandi Noir TV, but there are some elements of Nordic life that, no matter how appealing, simply will not work outside of their home countries. Here are the aspects of Scandi living that you've got no chance of being able to pull off.

CHIC CYCLING

Bet you didn't know a mode of transport could be hygge, did you? Or, if you did, you probably imagined aristocratic fur-lined highway carriages and Orient Express-esque train sleepovers. You definitely didn't conjure up images of a common or garden pushbike without even the slightest hint of a sheepskin saddle or hurricane-lantern lighting system. However, in Scandinavia cycling is the hygge-est way of all to get from A to B (with A being your laboratory-white loft apartment and B being your job in a concept design store that only sells five things).

The thing about chic cycling is that, yep, it's all very well when you're riding on excellently maintained, quiet, super-clean streets in pleasantly cool temperatures, but

it's less stylish when you've got to plough through road-blocking dams of chicken boxes and sink-hole-esque tarmac. Dashing in to work on your natty little retro boneshaker is a positive delight when you've got office bathroom facilities that'd score a 4.5 on TripAdvisor. Lining up for the one shower in your office of 350 people, where the water pressure you could only describe as "severely enlarged prostate," is not so delightful.

There's also something about Nordic hair that doesn't fall prey to helmet head. Maybe the Vikings had stronger follicles or something, but there's not a hint of clammy and wispy as they glamorously whip off their ergonomic protection, just a sweeping curtain of shampoo-ad gorgeousness. And forget embarrassing Lycra that adds inches

where you don't want it, and takes them away from where you do (as any man who's ever worn cycling shorts and a non-groin-covering top will testify), chic skinny trousers and an all-weather fabric turtleneck are the perfect Scandi cycling uniform.

EXTENDED MATERNITY/PATERNITY LEAVE

No one quite knows why, but for some reason the Nordics are world leaders in maternity and paternity leave. Maybe it's 'cos it's dark a lot of the time and the government realize people have no choice but to stay in and make potential babies. Therefore the authorities make things as easy as possible for those that get knocked up/are part of the knocking-up process. In Sweden, new parents get 480 days of leave and dads get another 90 days for bonding with their child, while Norway gives its residents around 56 weeks and Danes get a year. Do you know what you get? If the answer is "I think you're allowed to leave the office to have the baby/drive the person having the baby to the hospital for the birth," then moving to a Nordic country purely for the purpose of procreation sounds like a pretty good bet.

LEAVING WORK AT 4PM

Hang on a minute, so the Scandis get until the kids are practically in puberty for mat/pat leave AND they finish work at 4pm? Ummm... How does anything ever get done? Nordics believe a work-life balance to be important; and they use these extra two hours at the end of the day to do wholesome family activities like swim in a lake, have a picnic outdoors, or go for an early evening hike. Hmmm. You know what you'd do if you finished two hours earlier? You'd go for a drink. So really your miserable company is doing you a favor, for were they to adopt Scandi-esque hours, your liver probably couldn't take it.

BEING NAKED IN A SAUNA

You'd love to be free and continental, but you know everyone will look at you like you're a pervert. Plus, the grubby-looking sweatbox at Pay4U Gym isn't exactly a window looking out on the edge of a lake, architecturally acclaimed experience. Oh, and your fellow sauna inhabitees are not likely to be toned, flawless, striding Scandi beauties and you kind of don't want to encourage 'Roid Rage Pete or Zumba Helps Me With My Menopause Symptoms Jean to shed all. Best keep your swimmers on, hey?

EATING FISH AT YOUR DESK

There are a lot of things you can say about Nordic cuisine, but regardless of whether you are a lover or a hater of the way they do food, there's one thing you can't deny... A lot of it stinks. Healthy and as fashionable as your little brown paper-wrapped, mason-jar-enclosed, on-trend, New-Nordic-recipe pickled herring may be, you know anything fishier than a prawn cracker eaten in close proximity to your colleagues—ESPECIALLY if a microwave is involved—will have you taking over in a flash from Ken-who-never-puts-any-money-into-the-birthday-collections as the office's most hated person. Save the fish consumption for your own home, but be warned: the scent of cured fish is a nightmare to shift from faux fur.

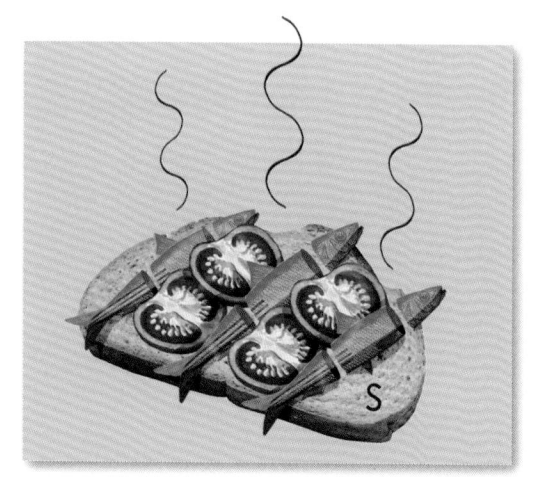

WHAT NEXT FOR NORDIC FANS?

OK, even the most die-hard fans of folk-art blankets and expensive artisanal hot chocolate have to admit that hygge is a little, shall we say, over-exposed. And if there's one thing a Scandinavian really can't risk it's exposure; you'll have hypothermia in a jiffy. Also, as discussed previously, we're just not sure lagom is gonna be our thing. So what new word that we don't know how to pronounce correctly can we rely on to act as snazzy little shorthand that we're absolutely on top of current lifestyle trends? Don't worry, there are plenty more where hygge came from. Here's a selection of what words might be coming and our odds on which may take the crown and become the next big thing.

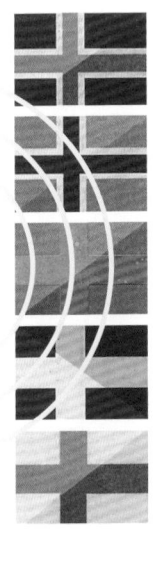

Word: *FIKA*

Nationality: Swedish

Meaning: The act of taking a coffee break with friends or coworkers. Frequently involves pastries.

Odds—3/1: It's pretty much a sure thing that *fika* will soon start making its way into the lexicon of your "cooler" pals. A strong contender for brunch in the smug weekend Instagram category, expect bottomless or all-you-can-eat *fika* pop-ups to start darkening your high streets any day now. The non-Scandi workplace might be a trickier environment for this trend to assimilate itself into, though. Non-Nordic bosses tend to not really like having to pay for lengthy toilet breaks, let alone cracking open the choccy croissants at 3pm every day and stopping work for half an hour.

Word: *MORGENFRISK*
Nationality: Danish
Meaning: The feeling of being refreshed in the morning after a great night's sleep.
Odds—2/1: This is an advertisers dream. *Morgenfrisk* will soon be used to sell everything from Viagra (in fact, what a great name for an erectile dysfunction drug—can we patent this please?) to those annoying mattresses that you can unroll but don't have to pay for if you don't like them after a 100-day trial or something. (Why is it that adverts for these hipster mattress companies are all we see on Facebook at the moment. When did even our mattresses have to be marketed to us like they should come in a mason jar?). We bet you can predict the person in your friendship circle who will first write "#morgenfrisk." Their social-media message will probably be posted two hours before your alarm has even gone off and it will almost definitely be a post-yoga selfie. Ugh.

Word: *FORELSKET*
Nationality: Norwegian
Meaning: The joy felt when you start to fall in love.
Odds—8/1: The main problem with *forelsket* is it doesn't sound very romantic. Instead of conjuring up images of first kisses in front of romantic sunsets, it does kind of sound like the sort of thing you'd shout to ward off a load of foxes going through your bins at 3am or something

you'd be called in a foreign bar when you accidentally spilt the tankard of Carlsberg belonging to the scary-looking bloke to your left. Nice concept, but bad aural effect. Sorry Norway.

Word: *GLUGGAVEÐUR*

Nationality: Iceland

Meaning: Window weather.

Odds—6/2 (yeah, we know odds of 6/2 is the same as 3/1—we think—but it's dull putting everything as the second favorite): *Gluggaveður* is definitely coming to an interiors blog near you, summing up the feeling of "oh, that snow storm's nice to look at, but I wouldn't want to be actually in the thick of it." This sounds a bit like fake breasts, or other people's family holidays. It's the perfect lifestyle trend for lazy people and thus perfect for us. To embrace it is easy peasy; literally all you have to do is stay in on the sofa, lie under a blanket (of course, hygge gets its greedy little fur-lined mitts in there somewhere), and occasionally look up from the TV to a window. And if you really want to commit to *gluggaveður*, then a couple of succulents on the windowsill or some vaguely forest-themed curtains will mark you out as an early adopter.

Word: *BAGSTIV*

Nationality: Danish

Meaning: Waking up still drunk from the night before.

Odds—5/1: Are we sure we don't already have this saying in English? This sounds

like exactly the kind of thing red-trouser wearing Randolphs and deck-shoe sporting Jezs would say after a night on the beers. Visit any rowing club/trading floor/dominatrix dungeon (come on, it's always posh preppy boys wanting to recreate nanny giving them a good spanking) and the chances of hearing "Hells bells, old boy! I was absolutely *bagstived* this morning," seem pretty high.

Word: *BUKSVÅGER*

Nationality: Swedish

Meaning: A person who has slept with someone you've slept with.

Odds—7/1: Now this word is genuinely useful, because currently we have to make do with one of the following: "slut" if you are/were sleeping with the person at the time, or "ex" if you're trying to be polite. As such, *buksvåger* presents a much better option when speaking about a former fling than your usual method, where you frostily mispronounce their name slightly in order to subtly convey your feeling of distaste. "Oh Ca-THE-rine is going to be there is she? How nice..."

Word: *ROMJUL*

Nationality: Norwegian

Meaning: The period between Christmas and New Year when you do nothing.

Odds—2/1: When it comes to new lifestyle trends, interior experts are suckers for anything a bit Emperor's New Clothes-y. If you think about it, when your job is to write in reverential tones usually reserved for the possibility of the Second Coming about sofas—on which one does little but sit—or walls—which kind of have to be there to hold your roof up—then you can see how a fresh way to re-package something that everyone already does anyway sounds enticing. So you can thank lifestyle journalists for the fact that doing absolutely nothing following an excess of food, booze, and family when you're in no way fit to be seen by the outside world can now be considered a bona fide style choice! Eating chocolate and Christmas cookie sandwiches? Totally *romjul*. Not wearing a bra for 72 hours? *Romjul* as hell. Wondering what that woman in the movie *Room* was so desperate to get away from when the thought of living indoors for the rest of your life feels so very perfect? King of *romjul*.

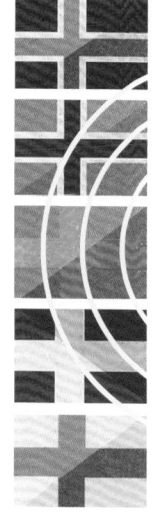

INDEX

& Other Stories 13
A-ha 18-19
ABBA 10, 18, 24
Ace of Base 18
alcohol 30, 34-35, 62
Alphabeat 19
Andersen, Hans Christian 26
antlers 49-50
Aqua 19
Avicii 19

baby welcome kits 30
backpacks 14-15
bagstiv 62
bandy (winter sport) 36
baskets 42
Basshunter 19
Björk 19
body cookies 43
Borg, Björn 25
buksvåger 62

cacti 50
candles 41, 49, 50
The Cardigans 19
Cheap Monday 13
Christmas 30, 62
clothing 12-13, 16-17
cloudberries 43
copper 50
Cos 12
cost of living 35
cycling 56-58

driving 31

Ericsson phones 39
Europe (rock band) 20
Eurovision Song Contest 20, 34

faux fur 41, 59
fika 60
floor cushions 42
Flying Jacob casserole 45
Flying Tiger store 50
food 43-45, 59
forelsket 61-62

Garbo, Greta 28
gluggaveður 62

H & M 12-13
hobbies 36-37
hygge 40-42, 46, 47, 56, 60

ice-white hair 22-23
icons 24-29
IKEA 39, 41, 43, 47
interior design 41-42, 48-51

Johansson, Scarlett 29
Joulupukki 30

lagom 46-47
lifestyle trends 60-63
lingonberries 43
Longstocking, Pippi 27, 28
Lund, Sarah 24

Malm beds 39
maternity/paternity leave 58
Mikkelsen, Mads 25
Monki 13
morgenfrisk 61
music 18-21

Nokia phones 38
Nordic Noir 54-55
nudity 33-34, 59

pendant lighting 48-49
penguins 31
phone throwing 37

quizzes 10-11, 30-31

Rednex 20
romjul 62-63
Roxette 20

Salander, Lisbeth 27
saunas 11, 33-34, 36, 59
Scandinavia 31
sex 35, 52
sheepskin 50
singletons 31
Skarsgård, Alexander 24, 33
Skype 39
snoods 16, 17
sour milk 45
surströmming 44-45
Swedish Chef (Muppet) 35
Swedish House Mafia 20-21
sweets 45

taxes 10, 32-33
Thor 29
trolls and troll dolls 27, 31
turtlenecks 17, 58
TV 35, 54-55

Volvos 38

weather 33, 62
Weekday 12
Whigfield 21
white floorboards 48
wife carrying 37
wood piles 42
work-life balance 58
workplace 58, 60